A Written Word

Tammy McNee

BookLeaf Publishing

India | USA | UK

Presentation by *BookLeaf Publishing*

Web: www.bookleafpub.com

E-mail: info@bookleafpub.com

ISBN : 9789357448215

First edition 2021

DEDICATION

To 17 year old me

You will be okay

Promise

ACKNOWLEDGEMENT

Ever since I can remember I've always wanted to write my own book. I always thought it would be a novel but I always doubted I could write something so magnificent and magical. When this opportunity came up, there was no way I could refuse. So firstly, thank you to my beautiful client turned friend Kat for sharing this with me, I'll be forever grateful.

Thank you to my Mum and Dad for a wonderful childhood full of books and magazines and a place to explore all my creative urges. I still remember my first journal and writing letters whenever I wanted something that I was too embarrassed to ask for! I thank you both, for your endless support.

Thank you to my beautiful best friend Melissa. If it wasn't for your encouragement and belief in me I wouldn't be sharing my words with anyone. You have this insane amount of passion and determination and it makes me so proud to see you fight for what you want and the people you love. You have a heart of gold and I am so grateful for you and our friendship. Thank you for always believing in me.

A huge thank you to Shannon. You are so wise, so so wise. Your perspective on life has taught me that its up to us and only us to change the way we think. Always putting others first, you love hard and I am blessed to be apart of that. Thank you for your support and for teaching me to be kinder to myself.

You and Melissa are two of the most supporting and kind people in my life and everyday I am so grateful. There is a poem in here dedicated to you both- I hope you find it!

To my partner- Joshua. Ugh, I love you. So much. I have a lot I could say but I will keep it as short as I can. You amaze me, everyday. With your strength, your drive, your go go go attitude towards life and your love. Thank you for protecting me and making me feel safe, thank you for always listening and loving me no matter what. Thank you for making me laugh and making life fun and bright. Thank you for never giving up on me. And thank you for being my person.

To every other beautiful person in my life- my family, Joshua's family and my friends- I love you all.

To the clients that have become friends, thankyou

The people in my life I share my books with, Danielle and Franca - special mention, thats a connection I'll always cherish.

And lastly to Trent Dalton - if this book every lands in your hands, I'm done. My life would be complete. Your books changed things for me and I will never forget the impact they've had on my life. Thank you for your magic.

PREFACE

Writing has changed my life for the better. It helps me to explain my thoughts when my voice cannot. It helps me to connect with others and share my experiences. I may be young but my love for words has been with me for a long time and I hope it continues to stay with me for years to come.

THE GIRL WITH TWO SELVES

looking into a mirror at your reflection
do you recognise her?
she's blonde, with freckle covered skin, pale
blue eyes
she feels loved and abundant
golden and radiant
did you see that? her eyes are glassy, full of tears
the pale blue turning to a dark navy
her hearts weighing down in her chest
creating a hunch in her shoulders, steps getting
heavier and heavier
she's a new person to you
the mirror looks darker, the corners dragging in
do you recognise her now?
she is still you
she thinks in black and white
theres no yellow brick road for her to follow
holding the weight of her thoughts on her back
she's blonde, with freckle covered skin, pale
blue eyes
hold her hand
hold it tight and help her pave her own road

for she is you
and you are her
a soul split into two
a gemini

THE CLOUDS

the veins in the clouds on a stormy day
speak to me
they say
"dear, its okay to feel sad, let it touch your skin
like the wind,
cold and sharp
but make sure to let it go, back into the sky
where it cannot hurt you"
leaving no scars behind

FORGOTTEN

theres a chunk of my life that seems missing
from my memories
scars on my body
that I know weren't from grazing my knees as a
kid
or from a branch while climbing through the
trees
no
these happened when I was a little bit older
when I thought that my life was over
because
well
I don't know why
how silly of me to think that life was over
I had a monster inside my chest, clawing
through my body
leaving scratches and scars on its way
feeding me lies, dragging me down a black hole
It looked so inviting, I was being heard, finally!
those sharp objects seemed exciting
You ARE depressed, YOU ARE RIGHT, you
DO hate yourself, pick it up
I have the white lines on my body, proving to me
it happened
but

Why don't I remember this now, ten years later?
Is this even my story to tell or am I telling
someone else's?
When did this monster leave me?
I remember feeling heavy, like I was carrying a
boulder all day
and those sharp objects helped me to let it go
until
it was time to pick it up again
What was my why?

"I'm just trying to protect you" my brain says
"We don't need to remember
the monster is gone
we no longer think that way
that boulder was crushed
you decided to love yourself.
That's all we need to remember"
I am safe now.

ANXIETY

it makes you selfish
the mind speaks to you as if everything around
you is crumbling
that you are the reason for every humans bad
mood
or every bad thing in your world
and because its obviously your fault you need to
fix it
as quickly as possible
because if you don't that person will leave you
and you'll be forgotten
and now you spiral
this spiral makes you panic
that you are not loved
that you're a fuck up
because only fuck ups are as unloved and
unworthy as you are
then you realise that you're overthinking
so you try to rationalise your thoughts
"maybe they just had a bad day, maybe its not
my fault"
but that part of your brain pushes those
productive thoughts away
"its absolutely your fault, remember?"
oh yes how silly of me to forget

someone called you selfish once
for thinking everything revolves around you
that memory popping into your head
yes I am being selfish
and that's when you realise
they got every red light on the way home
they received bad news at work
they are tired
your anxiety sent you into a panic before you
could even ask
"how was your day?"

EXIST

I've wanted to up and disappear many times
vanish into thin air
not in the way you may be thinking
I've never wanted to un alive myself, pinky
promise
but the thought of not existing, like I'm not
really here
you know when you pop a bubble and its gone?
yeah, that
have all my worries and problems come with me
have every hurtful thing I've said, every mistake,
gone
leave all the expectations and pressures behind
I don't want anyone to hurt
so I want everyone in my life to keep on living
as if nothings happened
It's not that I wouldn't be alive because my soul
doesn't exist
no one would be upset because they wouldn't
even know
because I wouldn't exist, you following?
BUT
if I didn't exist, my partner wouldn't know how
loved he is

how proud I am of him
Bella would be left without her human friend
my best friends wouldn't have someone to drink
endless coffee or wine with
someone to laugh with until we cry or cry until
we laugh
my neighbour wouldn't have someone to help
count his baby cows every spring
my parents wouldn't have a daughter
and my brothers wouldn't have a sister
if I didn't exist
I wouldn't be able to see the beauty in the world
when others can't
I wouldn't be using my words for good, I
wouldn't grow
I'd stop thinking in colour, I'd stop thinking at all
and as much as I despise my mind for these
thoughts
I remember
that we have 6000 thoughts a day
80% of those are negative
they are an idea or opinion produced by
thinking, not always reality
sometimes
I wish I would unscrew my brain
place it in warm water in a safe place
so my heart can take a break from the voices
It's so loud in my head sometimes
so when I say I don't wish to exist

I just wish for a break from all the noise.

YOUR EYES

its known that our eyes are the windows to the
soul
they are the portal to our deepest secrets
so tell me, can you lie to me while your eyes
expose your truth?

the way they change to the deepest shade of blue
pupils dilated as dark as the night sky
when you're staring into the ones who hold your
heart
as if they were your drug and you were taking
all the pills at once

when you're crying and have cleansed your eyes
with your pain
they are as blue as the ocean on a sunny day
the wetness of your tears illuminating the
freckles on your skin

when you're filled with despair, confused, lost
just grey, cloudy and lifeless

the eyes speak a language we can't comprehend
they tell our secrets to whoever dares to listen
no point in lying

when you're looking through the windows

12

HELLO MOON

I beg of the moon
to help me
I've laid out my crystals
I've done the assignments
did I pass?

oh I hope I passed your lessons

I AM YELLOW

when I told him he was blue
he said he didn't understand
blue like the ocean, sometimes bright and clear
sometimes hazy and secretive
but so calming, so free, moving in sync with the
sky
I explained
when I see her, she's red, filled with passion and
drive
with a roar like a lion
so much strength, so much energy to give
are you following? I say
I said, she's purple
fiercely protective, with wisdom beyond her
years
a magical soul, deep connections

and me? You ask
I am yellow

LONGWARRY

the first kiss, after sleep
the smile that's bursting between your lips
a mix between morning breath and pure delight
bodies touching as you slowly wake
sunshine peeking through the blinds
coffee brewing, brought to you in bed
caffeine stimulating all your senses
you smile to yourself, bliss
the sound of nature, awake for hours already
while you were dreaming
a mind full of wonder
watching the world rotate as you immerse
yourself into a book
the day goes on, you hear the cows, hungry for
hay
the midday train rattling past
he smells like freshly mowed grass and sweat
you breath it all in
sun setting over the paddocks
you watch from your kitchen window
the sky going through its daily transformation
from day to night
the first star shines bright and the moon makes
its appearance

heart and belly full
the meeting of two waters
my home, Longwarry

HOME

I find my home in people
I hope one day I can find a home within myself

GEMINI

ruled by mercury
she is wise and curious
mind full of questions
she is the sign of duality
contrasting, like day and night
she is mysterious
her passions kept private
made from a combination of
raw magic and wild spirit
she is capable of love like no other
her eyes are the windows
unable to hide emoiton
she is the sun over an open field
find a place in her heart and you are safe
she's a challenge
a soul split into two
but she is so worth it

SHE IS

when she is small, colourless
when she grows, her colours spread like wildfire

when she uses her voice, she's lying
when she is silence, honesty

she speaks to be heard
believe me
colours splashing the pavement

her words are not heard
there is no voice
she is colourless

VULVA

the ins and outs of the vulva
so soft to the touch, so pretty to explore
touch her gently, hear her response
what makes her toes curl?
her breathing louder, her voice quiver

SEX

our bodies move as one
every touch like sparks from a flame
exploding into my body
rippling
melting into your lips
gasping for breath
wrapping my body in your warmth
pulling you closer
I'm addicted to your taste
reaching the climax together
begging to come
I'm all yours

ORGASM

my hands rubbing between my thighs
knowing exactly where to touch, gentle at first
then with purpose
my body in rhythm with my pulse
my mind so removed, out of body
so deeply present
moans releasing from my mouth
uncontrolled and intense
my hands listening to my breath
knowing what feels good
the heated touch connecting with the richest part
of my body
sending shock waves down my legs
my body submits to the orgasm
letting my clit take the reigns
making my pussy come
all eight thousand nerve endings colliding
exploding, pulsing, throbbing
leaving me breathless and wet
feeling euphoric

SWEET

sweet nectar
dripping from their lips

"you taste so sweet"
they say
slipping deep inside you

A NEW DAY

let the sun set
over today
turning into yesterday
when the sun rises again
rise with it
shower away the thoughts
of the past
welcome the smell
of a new day
brush away the sadness
for today is new
and today has hope
and today feels a little more beautiful
because its one day closer to you

MY BODY

the softness of her breasts when she has just
woken
her nipples glazed over
aroused by your touch
goosebumps moving from head to toe
her naked body
perfectly imperfect
all those little scars and stretches
a piece of art you never want to finish
hips that remind you of the ocean
your hands fitting alongside her waist
giving comfort
females are fucking beautiful
they are more than their body
but their bodies
so beautiful
are deserving of your worship

MAN OF FIRE-
ARIES

ruled by mars
a hunter
with powerful energies of a Ram
chasing freedom and success
he is confident
he is direct
a huge heart with only love to give
hidden underneath that independent exterior
moving mountains without fear
a passionate and courageous lover
charming and mischievous
the leader of the herd
the alpha male

THE FIRE TO MY AIR

the fire to my air
picked me up from a broken place
they wrapped me in a cocoon of love
allowing me to transform
until I was ready to emerge
full of love and light

the holder of my heart
who spent his childhood
creating havoc
being adventurous
courageous and daring

taught me to be strong
speak my voice even if it shakes
he is giving me the life
I always dreamed
a little white cottage
that we've made our own

little inside jokes, secrets
made only for us

and when I look at him
eyes golden brown
my heart explodes

because to love someone is a gift
and I am beyond spoilt

MAY I HAVE THE LAST WORD

and now we're at the end
where there is no end
just another door open wide
the brightest of yellow welcoming you
with the warmest of arms
well done poss
you did it